W9-CBZ-498

Team Spirit • College Football

The Florida Gators®

BY
MARK STEWART

Content Consultant
Kent Stephens
College Football Hall of Fame

NORWOOD HOUSE PRESS
CHICAGO, ILLINOIS

Norwood House Press
P.O. Box 316598
Chicago, Illinois 60631

For information regarding Norwood House Press, please visit our website at:
www.norwoodhousepress.com or call 866-565-2900.

All photos courtesy of Getty Images except the following:
Classic Games, Inc. (5, 37 left, 41 top right),
University of Florida (6, 15, 17, 31, 34, 36 left, 37 top right, 39, 41 bottom left),
Playoff Corp. (9), Street & Smith's Sports Group (14, 21),
Associated Press (18, 19, 26, and 37 bottom), Hoby Cards, Inc. (22, 24, 38),
Fleer/SkyBox Intl. (25), Author's Collection (23, 33, 40), Downtown Athletic Club of NYC, Inc. (36),
SA•GE Collectibles, Inc. (41 bottom right), Matt Richman (48).
Cover Photo: Doug Benc/Getty Images

Special thanks to Topps, Inc.

Editor: Mike Kennedy
Designer: Ron Jaffe
Project Management: Black Book Partners, LLC.
Editorial Production: Jessica McCulloch
Research: Joshua Zaffos
Special thanks to Jason Ringdahl

Library of Congress Cataloging-in-Publication Data

Stewart, Mark, 1960-
   The Florida Gators / by Mark Stewart.
      p. cm. -- (Team spirit--college football)
   Includes bibliographical references and index.
   Summary: "Presents the history and accomplishments of the University of
Florida Gators football team. Includes highlights of players, coaches, and
awards, longstanding rivalries, quotes, timeline, maps, glossary and
websites"--Provided by publisher.
   ISBN-13: 978-1-59953-333-9 (library edition : alk. paper)
   ISBN-10: 1-59953-333-2 (library edition : alk. paper)
   1. University of Florida--Football--Juvenile literature. 2. Florida
Gators (Football team)--Juvenile literature. I. Title.
   GV958.U523S84 2010
   796.332'630975979--dc22
                                              2009029553

Manufactured in the United States of America in North Mankato, Minnesota.
159N—072010

COVER PHOTO: The Gators celebrate after a victory during the 2005 season.

Table of Contents

SPORTS WORDS & VOCABULARY WORDS: In this book, you will find many words that are new to you. You may also see familiar words used in new ways. The glossary on page 46 gives the meanings of football words, as well as "everyday" words that have special football meanings. These words appear in **bold type** throughout the book. The glossary on page 47 gives the meanings of vocabulary words that are not related to football. They appear in ***bold italic type*** throughout the book.

Meet the Gators

When most Americans think of Florida, they picture bright sunshine, warm breezes, swaying palm trees, and clear water. For many people, there is no place they would rather be. For college football players, the scene is very different. Florida means playing in the "Swamp" and getting chomped by "Gators."

The University of Florida is one of the most popular colleges in the United States. It has won national championships in basketball, track, swimming, golf, tennis, and soccer. During the first half of every school year, however, the big sport on the Gainesville campus is football. The Gators often challenge for the national title.

This book tells the story of the Florida Gators. For many years, the team played mostly to entertain its fans. But once the winning started, football became serious business to the school's millions of supporters. Over the years, the Gators have found a way to make the sport a little of both. To Florida's players, playing championship football is serious fun.

The Gators celebrate a touchdown during the 2001 season.

5

Way Back When

The first Florida football team suited up in 1906. The school's first star was an acrobatic receiver named Dale Van Sickel, who played in the 1920s. He would later become famous as a movie stuntman. The team lost only six games during his three varsity seasons. The Gators joined the **Southeastern Conference (SEC)** in 1933 along with

powerful teams such as Auburn, Georgia, and Alabama. Against this kind of competition, Florida often struggled to win.

That changed when Bob Woodruff was hired to coach the team in 1950. Lineman Charlie LaPradd **anchored** the defense, and Rick Casares, John "Papa" Hall, and Buford Long led the rushing attack. In 1953, the Gators played in their first bowl game, the **Gator Bowl**. They beat Tulsa 14–13. Six seasons later, Florida played the first game of its long *rivalry* with Florida State. Quarterback Jimmy Dunn was the hero in an exciting victory.

Florida football really took off in the 1960s. The team built a great defense, while quarterback Steve Spurrier guided the offense. He specialized in *comeback* victories. In 1966, Spurrier won the **Heisman Trophy**. He did it all for the Gators—including kicking the winning **field goal** in a game against Auburn!

Florida had some great players during the 1970s and 1980s, including Sammy Green, Kerwin Bell, David Little, Wilber Marshall, and Louis Oliver. Lomas Brown was the cornerstone of a powerful offensive line that blocked for running backs John L. Williams and Neal Anderson. Emmitt Smith was Florida's most *dynamic* runner. He broke the school record for yards in a game in his first start. Smith was named an **All-American** two seasons later, in 1989.

In 1990, Spurrier returned to Gainesville as the team's coach. He turned the Gators into a great passing team with talented players like

LEFT: Bob Woodruff, one of the top coaches in school history.
ABOVE: A trading card of Emmitt Smith, one of the greatest runners in school history.

quarterback Danny Wuerffel and receivers Ike Hilliard and Reidel Anthony. Wuerffel threw 114 touchdown passes from 1993 to 1996—the second-most in college football history at that time. Spurrier also had excellent runners, including Errict Rhett and Fred Taylor.

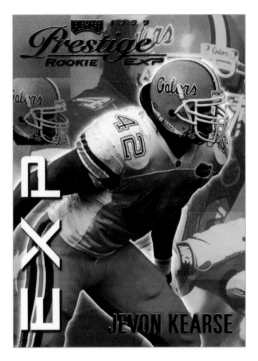

The Gators went through the 1995 schedule without a loss for the second time in school history. Their dreams of an *undefeated* season and a national title were ruined in the **Fiesta Bowl** when they lost to Nebraska. In 1996, the Gators bounced back. They went 12–1 and destroyed Florida State in the **Sugar Bowl** to finish the year as the national champions.

Although Spurrier was known as an offensive genius, the Gators also had one of the most fearsome defenses in the 1990s. More than 70 Florida linemen, linebackers, and defensive backs during the *decade* went on to play in the **National Football League (NFL)**. Spurrier left Florida in 2002, and the team struggled to beat the nation's top squads. The Gators needed a new leader to help them return to their championship form.

LEFT: Steve Spurrier and Danny Wuerffel discuss a play during the 1997 Sugar Bowl.   **ABOVE**: Jevon Kearse, one of the many defensive stars who played for Florida in the 1990s.

21st Century

The Gators hired Urban Meyer to coach the team in 2005. A year later, they took the **SEC Championship** and beat Ohio State in the title game in the **Bowl Championship Series (BCS)**. The team was led by quarterback Chris Leak and defensive stars Brandon Siler, Ray McDonald, Jarvis Moss, Ryan Smith, and Reggie Nelson. It was Florida's second national championship.

Meyer continued to build Florida into a powerhouse. He **recruited** top high school players, including quarterback Tim Tebow. In 2007, Tebow won the Heisman Trophy. A year later, he guided Florida to a victory over the Oklahoma Sooners for the national championship. The team's other leaders included two Brandons—James and Spikes—along with Phil Trautwein and Percy Harvin.

When Tebow announced that he would stay in school to play his senior season in 2009, Florida fans were thrilled. Few players have done more to uphold the school's great football *tradition*. Tebow and his teammates have set a standard of excellence on and off the field. With their example guiding future stars at Florida, the school should remain a powerhouse for years to come.

Tim Tebow and Urban Meyer talk on the sidelines during a 2008 game. Together, they helped make the Gators one of the nation's best teams.

Home Turf

The Gators play their home games in Ben Hill Griffin Stadium. Most college football fans know it as the Swamp. It is a difficult place for visiting teams to play. The stadium is steamy and noisy. It is also the largest in all of Florida. The Gators have gone through many seasons without losing a game on their home turf.

From 1971 to 1989, that turf was *artificial*. When it heated up in Florida's afternoon sun, it would become burning hot. In 1990, coach Steve Spurrier asked the school to change to grass—the original surface when the stadium was built in 1930. Spurrier later gave the field its nickname.

"The Swamp is where Gators live," he explained. "A swamp is hot, sticky, and dangerous." Opponents feel that way whenever they face Florida on its home field.

BY THE NUMBERS

- *The Swamp has 88,548 seats for football, though the Gators often draw crowds of more than 90,000.*
- *The original stadium had only 21,769 seats.*
- *In 2003 and 2004, the school spent more than $50 million to modernize the stadium.*

Ben Hill Griffin Stadium is alive with excitement for a 2007 game.

Dressed for Success

Florida's colors are orange and blue. The school has used some combination of these two colors almost every season for more than 90 years. Their current helmet is orange with *Gators* written in blue. For many years, the team used an *F* or *UF* instead.

At home games, the team wears blue jerseys with white numbers. When the Gators play on the road, they wear white jerseys with blue numbers. Their pants are either white or blue with an orange stripe.

Florida's **logo** features an alligator that the students call "Albert." Picking this **mascot** was an easy choice. There are more than one million alligators in Florida. During the 1990s, Albert looked like a cartoon character. Today, the Florida logo shows a fierce-looking alligator head against a blue and orange background.

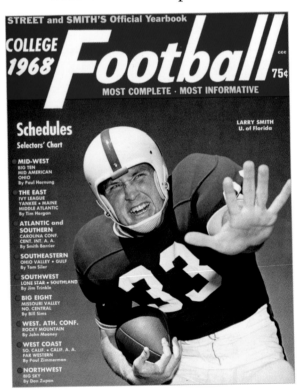

STREET and SMITH'S Official Yearbook

COLLEGE 1968

Football ccc

75¢

MOST COMPLETE · MOST INFORMATIVE

LARRY SMITH
U. of Florida

Schedules
Selectors' Chart

MID-WEST
BIG TEN
MID AMERICAN
OHIO
By Paul Hornung

THE EAST
IVY LEAGUE
YANKEE • MAINE
MIDDLE ATLANTIC
By Tim Horgan

ATLANTIC and SOUTHERN
CAROLINA CONF.
CENT. INT. A. A.
By Smith Barrier

SOUTHEASTERN
OHIO VALLEY • GULF
By Tom Siler

SOUTHWEST
LONE STAR • SOUTHLAND
By Jim Trinkle

BIG EIGHT
MISSOURI VALLEY
NO. CENTRAL
By Bill Sims

WEST. ATH. CONF.
ROCKY MOUNTAIN
By John Mooney

WEST COAST
SO. CALIF. • CALIF. A. A.
FAR WESTERN
By Paul Zimmerman

NORTHWEST
BIG SKY
By Don Zupan

Larry Smith models the Florida home uniform from the 1960s.

UNIFORM BASICS

The football uniform has three important parts—
- Helmet
- Jersey
- Pants

Helmets used to be made out of leather, and they did not have facemasks—ouch! Today, helmets are made of super-strong plastic. The uniform top, or jersey, is made of thick fabric. It fits snugly around a player so that tacklers cannot grab it and pull him down. The pants come down just over the knees.

There is a lot more to a football uniform than what you see on the outside. Air can be pumped inside the helmet to give it a snug, padded fit. The jersey covers shoulder pads, and sometimes a rib protector called a flak jacket. The pants include pads that protect the hips, thighs, *tailbone*, and knees.

Football teams have two sets of uniforms—one dark and one light. This makes it easier to tell two teams apart on the field. Almost all teams wear their dark uniforms at home and their light ones on the road.

Percy Harvin carries the ball wearing the team's 2008 road uniform.

We're Number 1!

Florida has been the unquestioned champion of college football three times, in 1996, 2006, and 2008. However, some say the school's 1984 squad was the best ever. Although Brigham Young University was recognized as the national champion that year, several publications—including *The Sporting News* and *The New York Times*—ranked the Gators as the country's top team. Unfortunately, Florida was found guilty of breaking recruiting rules, and the program was put on ***probation***.

The 1984 team was powered by freshman quarterback Kerwin Bell and runners Neal Anderson and John L. Williams. The secret to the Gators' success that season was a monstrous offensive line that featured Lomas Brown, Billy Hinson, Phil Bromley, Jeff Zimmerman, and Crawford Ker.

Florida's first undisputed national championship came in 1996. Quarterback Danny Wuerffel led the team to 12 victories. His favorite targets were Ike Hilliard, Reidel Anthony, and Jacquez Green. When the Gators needed tough yards on the ground, they handed the ball to Fred Taylor or Elijah Williams.

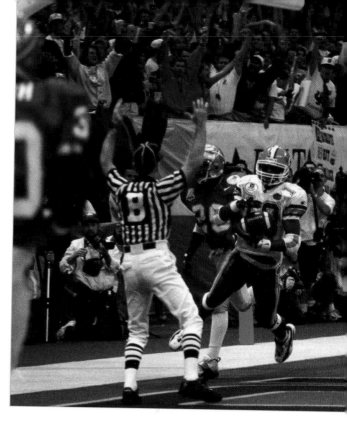

Florida fans celebrate after Ike Hilliard scores one of his three touchdowns during the 1997 Sugar Bowl.

Florida was the nation's top-ranked team until a heartbreaking loss to Florida State. The Gators bounced back to defeat Alabama in the SEC Championship, 45–30. Florida fans celebrated when they learned they would get a chance for revenge against Florida State in the Sugar Bowl!

The game was rough from start to finish. The Gators held a slim lead in the third quarter. That's when they really turned on the pressure. Florida exploded for four touchdowns in the second half to win 52–20. Wuerffel and Hilliard were the stars—they connected for touchdowns in the first, second, and third quarters.

In 2005, Urban Meyer was hired to coach the Gators. One year later, Florida was the conference champion. The Gators won the **SEC Eastern Division** and then defeated Arkansas in the SEC Championship. Quarterback Chris Leak and receivers Dallas Baker and Percy Harvin were the leaders on offense. When the game was

on the line, the defense took over. Earl Everett, Brandon Siler, Reggie Nelson, Ryan Smith, Jarvis Moss, and Derrick Harvey made big tackles and forced key **turnovers**.

The BCS Championship Game matched Florida with top-ranked Ohio State University. The contest started badly for the Gators when the Buckeyes ran back the opening kickoff for a touchdown. Leak and Baker answered with a touchdown of their own. From there, the defense took control. Ohio State scored just once more.

Florida, on the other hand, had no trouble moving the ball. The Gators used freshman Tim Tebow as a runner and passer. He was almost unstoppable. Tebow blasted through the line in the fourth quarter to make the final score 41–14. Leak played brilliantly and was named the **Most Valuable Player (MVP)** in the final game of his college career.

Two years later, the Gators were at it again. Tebow—the 2007 Heisman Trophy winner—threw 30 touchdown passes and ran for 792 yards. Florida won the SEC East and then played top-ranked Alabama for the conference championship. Florida was without Harvin, its talented runner and receiver. But Tebow had plenty of other targets. With the Gators trailing 20–17 in the fourth quarter, he seized control and led the team to a 31–20 victory—and a place in the BCS Championship Game against Oklahoma.

In that game, each team scored a touchdown in the first half. Florida took the lead in the third quarter on a trick play to Harvin, who was healthy and back in action. The Sooners tied the score 14–14 in the fourth quarter. After a 52-yard run by Harvin, Florida went ahead with a field goal. Tebow sealed the victory with a long drive that ended with a short touchdown pass. He finished with more than 200 passing yards and 100 rushing yards.

LEFT: Chris Leak raises the championship trophy after Florida's 2006 national title.   **ABOVE**: Percy Harvin jumps into the arms of Tim Tebow after his touchdown against Oklahoma.

Go-To Guys

STEVE SPURRIER   Quarterback

• BORN: 4/20/1945   • PLAYED FOR VARSITY: 1964–1966

Steve Spurrier could have been a basketball or baseball star. Luckily for the Gators, he chose football. Spurrier passed for 4,848 yards and 36 touchdowns during his college career. In 1966, he won the Heisman Trophy.

LARRY SMITH   Running Back

• BORN: 9/2/1947   • PLAYED FOR VARSITY: 1966–1968

Larry Smith led the Gators in rushing in all three of his varsity seasons. He was named an All-American as a senior and graduated as the school's all-time leading rusher. In the 1967 **Orange Bowl**, he gained 187 yards on 23 carries and was voted the game's MVP.

JOHN REAVES   Quarterback

• BORN: 3/2/1950   • PLAYED FOR VARSITY: 1969–1971

In his first game as a Gator, John Reaves broke Steve Spurrier's school record for passing yards. In his last game, he broke the **National Collegiate Athletic Association (NCAA)** career passing record. He won the Sammy Baugh Award as the top college passer in 1971.

LAWRENCE WRIGHT

Defensive Back

- BORN: 9/6/1973   • PLAYED FOR VARSITY: 1993–1996

Lawrence Wright was the captain of Florida's defense and the glue that held that unit together during the 1996 season. Wright was a hard hitter who always seemed to be in the right place at the right time. As a senior, he won the Jim Thorpe Award as the nation's top defensive back.

DANNY WUERFFEL

Quarterback

- BORN: 5/27/1974
- PLAYED FOR VARSITY: 1993–1996

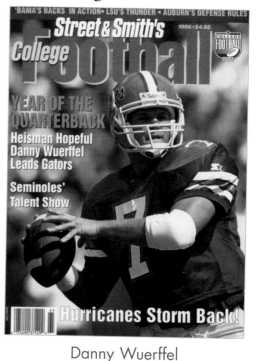

Danny Wuerffel

Danny Wuerffel was blessed with a strong arm and three great receivers—Reidel Anthony, Ike Hilliard, and Jacquez Green. During his four years as a starter, he led the Gators to four SEC titles. As a senior, he threw for 3,625 yards, led Florida to the national championship, and earned the Heisman Trophy.

TIM TEBOW

Quarterback

- BORN: 8/14/1987   • PLAYED FOR VARSITY: 2006–2009

Tim Tebow could do it all. As a junior, he broke the team record for rushing touchdowns in a season, passed for another 32 scores, and led the Gators to the national championship. That year, he won the Maxwell Award as the nation's best quarterback—but he did not win the Heisman Trophy. That was okay—he had won the award as a sophomore in 2007!

GAME BREAKERS

These great Gators were known for their game-changing plays!

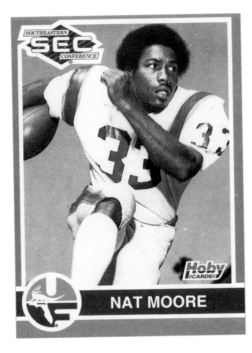

NAT MOORE

NAT MOORE   **Receiver**

- BORN: 9/19/1951
- PLAYED FOR VARSITY: 1972–1973

When Nat Moore was in the **lineup**, the Gators had a chance to score at any time. Despite being one of the smallest players on the team, Moore was tough and ***determined***. The speedy receiver ran his pass routes to perfection.

WES CHANDLER   **Receiver**

- BORN: 8/22/1956
- PLAYED FOR VARSITY: 1975–1977

The Gators liked to run the football when Wes Chandler was on the team. But that didn't stop him from ***dominating***. He averaged more than 20 yards per reception. During his career, Chandler caught 92 passes, scored 22 touchdowns, and was a two-time All-American.

CRIS COLLINSWORTH   **Receiver**

- BORN: 1/27/1959   • PLAYED FOR VARSITY: 1977–1980

Cris Collinsworth did not play receiver until he joined the Gators. In high school, he had been a quarterback and a state sprinting champion. Collinsworth used his great speed and fine hands to catch 120 passes for Florida, including 14 for touchdowns.

EMMITT SMITH
Running Back

• BORN: 5/15/1969 • PLAYED FOR VARSITY: 1987–1989

Emmitt Smith started his freshman year as a backup. He burst onto the scene in his first SEC game when he ran for 224 yards. Smith had 1,000 yards by his seventh game! When Smith left Florida for the NFL, he owned 58 school records.

ERRICT RHETT
Running Back

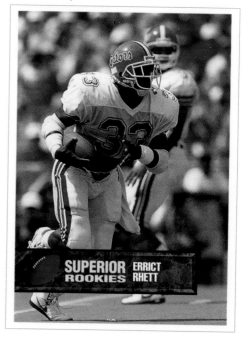

• BORN: 12/11/1970

• PLAYED FOR VARSITY: 1990–1993

The player who broke Emmitt Smith's career yardage record at Florida was Errict Rhett. He gained 4,163 yards and led the Gators in rushing in each of his four seasons. In his final college game—the 1994 Sugar Bowl— Rhett was named MVP as Florida rolled over West Virginia, 41–7.

FRED TAYLOR
Running Back

• BORN: 1/27/1976 • PLAYED FOR VARSITY: 1994–1997

Fred Taylor had the power and quickness to burst through openings of any size. Once he found running room, he could outrace everyone to the end zone. Taylor was a top runner on Florida's 1996 championship team. As a senior, he was named **All-SEC**.

LEFT: Nat Moore   **ABOVE**: Errict Rhett

RICK CASARES — Running Back

• BORN: 7/4/1931   • PLAYED FOR VARSITY: 1951–1953

Rick Casares stood taller than six feet, weighed more than 220 pounds, and was no fun to tackle. He was a track and basketball star who almost decided to become a boxer. As a junior, Casares led the Gators to their first bowl game.

JACK YOUNGBLOOD — Defensive Lineman

JACK YOUNGBLOOD

• BORN: 1/26/1950

• PLAYED FOR VARSITY: 1968–1970

When Jack Youngblood arrived at Florida, he was small and wiry. Over his career, he added extra muscle and became one of the greatest pass rushers in SEC history. Youngblood made headlines as a junior when he got five **sacks** in a game against Florida State.

LOMAS BROWN — Offensive Lineman

• BORN: 5/30/1963

• PLAYED FOR VARSITY: 1981–1984

In the SEC, offensive linemen have to be big, smart, and quick. Lomas Brown was all three—and then some. He anchored the team's amazing offensive line, which fans nicknamed the "Great Wall of Florida."

KEVIN CARTER   Defensive Lineman

- BORN: 9/21/1973   • PLAYED FOR VARSITY: 1991–1994

Kevin Carter was a force at defensive end for the Gators. When opposing quarterbacks dropped back to pass, they knew he would be on top of them in seconds. Carter was All-SEC in both his junior and senior years.

JEFF MITCHELL   Offensive Lineman

- BORN: 1/29/1974   • PLAYED FOR VARSITY: 1993–1996

Jeff Mitchell was the heart of the offensive line that protected Danny Wuerffel. He played alongside his friend Donnie Young, and the pair made it almost impossible for opponents to sack Wuerffel.

JEVON KEARSE   Linebacker

- BORN: 9/3/1976
- PLAYED FOR VARSITY: 1996–1998

Jevon Kearse was called the "Freak" because no one had ever seen such a big player move so quickly. He began his college career as a defensive back but moved to linebacker. Kearse helped the Gators win the national championship as a freshman and was SEC Defensive Player of the Year as a junior.

LEFT: Jack Youngblood   **ABOVE**: Jevon Kearse

On the Sidelines

The Gators have had many fine coaches over the years. Each moved the team forward and taught the players something new. The school's three most successful coaches were Ray Graves, Steve Spurrier, and Urban Meyer. Graves came to Gainesville in 1960 and brought a winning attitude to the team. He also began the tradition of building around star quarterbacks.

One of those quarterbacks was Spurrier, who returned to Florida as coach in 1990. He led the Gators to the SEC title in five of his first seven seasons. He also coached Florida to its first national title. Spurrier believed in developing a dangerous passing attack. That shook up the SEC, which had always favored the running game. Under Spurrier, the Gators became the first school to score 500 points in a season four years in a row. He won 122 games in 12 seasons.

In 2005, Florida fans welcomed Urban Meyer to Gainesville. Meyer taught his team the spread offense. This plan of attack made great use of Florida's speed and *agility*. Under Meyer, the Gators combined tricky running plays with short and long passes. This strategy paid off with two national championships in Meyer's first four seasons.

Urban Meyer signals a touchdown during Florida's win over Ohio State in the 2007 BCS Championship Game.

Rivals

When Florida joined the SEC in the 1930s, it developed three major rivals—Tennessee, Louisiana State, and Georgia. The game against Tennessee takes place early in the season every year. The Gators enjoyed their greatest run against the Volunteers from 1994 to 1997. Florida beat Tennessee and star quarterback Peyton Manning four years in a row. The Gators relied on athletic defensive stars such as Ellis Johnson, Kevin Carter, Ed Chester, and Jevon Kearse to confuse Manning and batter him with hard hits.

Georgia is a great rival of Florida because the two states are located next to each other. The game is played in Jacksonville, Florida, which is close to the Georgia border. The contest is the site of one of America's most famous tailgating parties.

Florida's greatest rival is Florida State. This game is usually scheduled for the end of the regular season. The schools began playing in 1958, but the rivalry reached a new level in the 1980s. By then, the Gators and Seminoles were ranked among the top teams in the nation.

When Florida squares off against Florida State, fans across the nation tune in to the game. Since Florida is known as the "Sunshine State," the contest has been nicknamed the "Sunshine Showdown."

Ed Chester takes down Peyton Manning in Florida's win over Tennessee in 1996.

Florida won 16 of the first 19 meetings between the schools. The teams tied in 1961 and 1994. In 1996, Florida was the nation's top team, and Florida State was second. One year later, the #10 Gators stunned the #1 Seminoles in their home stadium. Fred Taylor scored four touchdowns in that amazing comeback victory.

One Great Day

After Florida lost to Florida State in November of 1996, no one in Gainesville dreamed the Gators would be playing for the national championship. But a month later, they were doing exactly that. Florida again faced off against Florida State in the Sugar Bowl.

Gators coach Steve Spurrier knew the Seminoles well. This was his ninth game against Florida State, though he had only two wins to show for it. Still, Spurrier was confident. He had spotted a weakness in the Seminoles' great defense. He believed that his quarterback, Danny Wuerffel, would be able to take advantage of it.

Before the Sugar Bowl, Spurrier told Wuerffel to wait a second longer for his receivers to get open. Ike Hilliard used the extra time to explode past the Seminoles. Wuerffel hit him with a short touchdown pass in the first quarter and a long one in the second quarter. Florida led 24–20 in the third quarter when Wuerffel spotted Hilliard near the end zone. He "threaded the needle" with a pass between two defenders. Hilliard plucked the ball out of the air and dove across the goal line.

30

A happy and exhausted Danny Wuerffel waves to the crowd
after beating Florida State in the Sugar Bowl.

Moments later, Wuerffel dropped back to pass again. A group of Florida State tacklers raced after him. When Wuerffel took off down the field, the exhausted Seminoles were helpless to stop him. Wuerffel scored a touchdown to give Florida a huge lead. The Gators ended up winning 52–20. They were declared national champions.

"Danny did what he had to do," Spurrier remembers about that day. "He stood in there. Danny did it all. The whole team played super."

It Really Happened

In the long rivalry between Florida and Florida State, the best Sunshine Showdowns often come when both teams are playing their best. The most amazing game, however, came in October of 1971 when the Seminoles were undefeated and the Gators were winless.

A group of Florida players in their final season gathered on the field at midnight before the game. Two years earlier, they were known as the "Super Sophs." Running back Tommy Durrance gave an *inspiring* speech. His teammates were ready to shock the Seminoles!

Meanwhile, coach Doug Dickey decided to trick Florida State. Dickey knew the Seminoles would spend all week preparing for John Reaves, Florida's strong-armed quarterback. Dickey instructed his offense that it would run the football instead. This was quite a gamble—Florida had not scored a rushing touchdown all year long!

More than 65,000 fans watched in astonishment as Reaves handed off to Durrance and Mike Rich again and again. The Gators scored first on a run by Rich. Less than a minute later, Jimmy Barr scooped up a Florida State fumble and ran into the end zone to make the score 14–0.

The Seminoles cut the lead to 14–7 in the fourth quarter, but the Gators responded with a field goal. Florida State scored again and

An autographed photo of John Reaves, Florida's
leader in the early 1970s.

added a **two-point conversion**. Florida clung to a 17–15 lead and
played great defense to win the game. Reaves—who would go on to
capture the award as the nation's top quarterback—didn't throw a
single touchdown pass.

Team Spirit

Florida football fans have almost a century of traditions to follow. The most important is the Two-Bits Cheer, which goes, "Two bits, four bits, six bits, a dollar! All for the Gators, stand up and holler!" This is one of several cheers that Florida fans know—every student learns them during freshman *orientation*. Music is also an important tradition at Florida. After the third quarter at home games, students sing "We Are the Boys from Old Florida."

The team's main mascot is Albert the Alligator. During the 1950s, he was a real alligator. By the 1970s, Albert was played by a student in a costume. It is one of the hottest jobs in sports! In the 1980s, Albert was joined on the sidelines by Alberta, a female gator.

At the end of each season, one Florida senior player is picked to receive the Fergie Award. It is named after Forrest "Fergie" Ferguson, who was a great receiver for the team in the 1940s. Fergie was known for never giving up no matter how bad things looked. He fought in World War II and was awarded the Distinguished Service Cross for his bravery. He later died from his battle wounds. The Fergie Award recognizes the player who shows leadership, character, and courage.

Florida fans perform the "Gator Chomp," one of the team's many fun traditions.

Timeline

At the end of each college season, the best teams are invited to play in special "Bowl" games, such as the **Rose Bowl**, Orange Bowl, and Sugar Bowl. Bowl games usually take place in January, but they count in the final rankings of the previous season. That means the top team in 2008 wasn't decided until early 2009. In this timeline, bowl games are listed in the year they were held.

1906
The Gators play their first season.

1955
Don Chandler leads the nation in punting.

1915
Rammy Ramsdell is the first Gator to score four touchdowns in a game.

1953
Florida plays in the Gator Bowl.

1966
Steve Spurrier wins the Heisman Trophy.

Don Chandler

Steve Spurrier

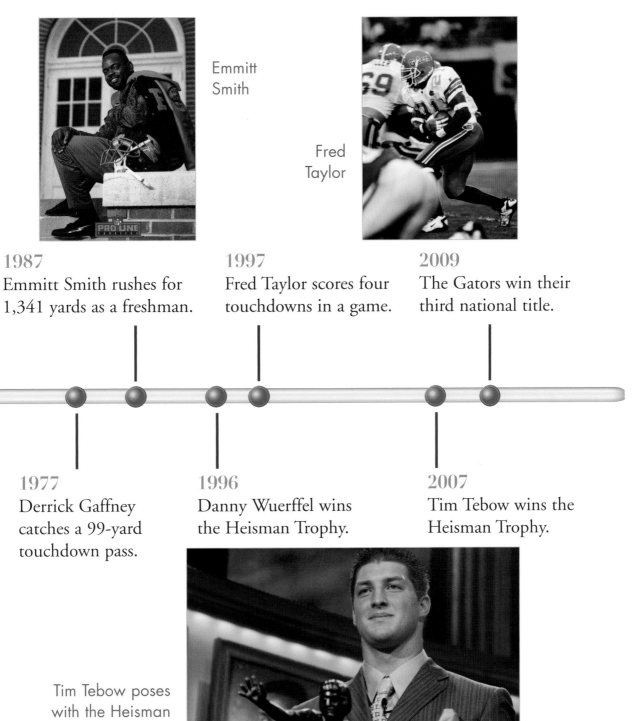

Emmitt Smith

Fred Taylor

1987
Emmitt Smith rushes for 1,341 yards as a freshman.

1997
Fred Taylor scores four touchdowns in a game.

2009
The Gators win their third national title.

1977
Derrick Gaffney catches a 99-yard touchdown pass.

1996
Danny Wuerffel wins the Heisman Trophy.

2007
Tim Tebow wins the Heisman Trophy.

Tim Tebow poses with the Heisman Trophy in 2007.

Fun Facts

GATOR POWER

During the 1960s, a scientist named Robert Cade asked Florida coach Ray Graves if he could test a new sports drink on his team. The players

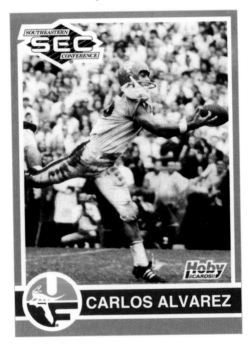

hated the taste, but they said the drink helped them play better. Dr. Cade made some adjustments to the *formula* and named the drink after the team: Gatorade.

THE CUBAN COMET

One of Florida's most exciting players was Carlos Alvarez. As a sophomore in 1969, he caught 88 passes to set a school record. Alvarez graduated in 1971 with more receiving yards than any player in school history.

HEARING RED

The first football game at the Swamp was played in November of 1930. The announcer that day was a student named Red Barber. He went on to become one of the most famous sportscasters in history.

THE MARSHALL PLAN

Wilber Marshall was one of the fastest, most powerful linebackers in the nation during the early 1980s. Gator fans often hung banners that read, "This Field Is Under Marshall Law."

JUST FOR KICKS

Jack Youngblood was one of the greatest defensive linemen in the history of college football. Florida fans also remember him as a talented kicker. In 1968, he booted a 42-yard field goal to beat Air Force.

YOU'RE SO NEGATIVE

Defense has always been the name of the game for the Gators. Their best performance came against Arkansas in 1997. When the final gun sounded, the Razorbacks had −56 rushing yards!

LEFT: A trading card shows Carlos Alvarez making a great catch.
ABOVE: Wilber Marshall takes down an opposing quarterback.

For the Record

The great Gators teams and players have left their marks on the record books. These are the "best of the best" …

GATORS AWARD WINNERS

JIM THORPE AWARD
TOP DEFENSIVE BACK

Lawrence Wright   1996

HEISMAN TROPHY
TOP COLLEGE PLAYER

Steve Spurrier	1966
Danny Wuerffel	1996
Tim Tebow	2007

WALTER CAMP AWARD
TOP COLLEGE PLAYER

Danny Wuerffel   1996

MAXWELL AWARD
TOP COLLEGE PLAYER

Danny Wuerffel	1996
Tim Tebow	2007
Tim Tebow	2008

DAVEY O'BRIEN AWARD
TOP QUARTERBACK

Danny Wuerffel	1995
Danny Wuerffel	1996
Tim Tebow	2007

JOHNNY UNITAS GOLDEN ARM AWARD
TOP SENIOR QUARTERBACK

Danny Wuerffel   1996

SAMMY BAUGH TROPHY
TOP COLLEGE PASSER

John Reaves	1971
Danny Wuerffel	1995

LOU GROZA AWARD
TOP PLACEKICKER

Judd Davis   1993

A pennant celebrating Florida's trip to the Sugar Bowl in 1966.

GATORS ACHIEVEMENTS

ACHIEVEMENT	YEAR
SEC Champions*	1984
Nationals Champions*	1984
SEC Champions*	1985
SEC Champions*	1990
SEC Champions	1991
SEC Champions	1993
SEC Champions	1994
SEC Champions	1995
SEC Champions	1996
Nationals Champions	1996
SEC Champions	2000
SEC Champions	2006
Nationals Champions	2006
SEC Champions	2008
Nationals Champions	2008

Title taken away because of rules violation.

SHANE MATTHEWS — QB

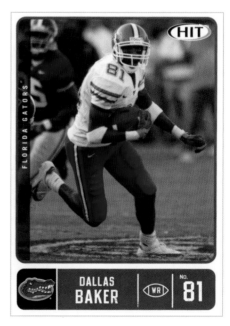

DALLAS BAKER — WR — NO. 81

ABOVE: John L. Williams, a star runner for the 1984 champs.
TOP RIGHT: Shane Matthews, the quarterback for the 1991 team.
BOTTOM RIGHT: Dallas Baker, a leader for the 2006 champs.

The SEC

The University of Florida is a member of the Southeastern Conference. The SEC was formed in 1932. There are 12 teams in the SEC. Florida plays in the Eastern Division of the SEC. These are Florida's neighbors …

THE SOUTHEASTERN CONFERENCE

EASTERN DIVISION

1   University of Florida Gators
       Gainesville, Florida

2   University of Georgia Bulldogs
       Athens, Georgia

3   University of Kentucky Wildcats
       Lexington, Kentucky

4   University of South Carolina Gamecocks
       Columbia, South Carolina

5   University of Tennessee Volunteers
       Knoxville, Tennessee

6   Vanderbilt University Commodores
       Nashville, Tennessee

WESTERN DIVISION

7   University of Alabama Crimson Tide
       Tuscaloosa, Alabama

8   University of Arkansas Razorbacks
       Fayetteville, Arkansas

9   Auburn University Tigers
       Auburn, Alabama

10 Louisiana State University Tigers
       Baton Rouge, Louisiana

11 University of Mississippi Rebels
       Oxford, Mississippi

12 Mississippi State University Bulldogs
       Starkville, Mississippi

The College Game

College football may look like the same game you see NFL teams play on Sundays, but there are some important differences. The first is that most college games take place on Saturday. This has been true for more than 100 years. Below are several other differences between college and pro football.

CLASS NOTES

College players are younger than NFL players. They are student-athletes who have graduated from high school and now play on their college's varsity team, which is the highest level of competition. Most are between the ages of 18 and 22.

College players are allowed to compete for four seasons. Each year is given a different name, or "class"—freshman (first year), sophomore (second year), junior (third year), and senior (fourth year). Players who are unable to play for the varsity can remain in the same class for an extra year. This is called "red-shirting." These players are still students and must attend classes during their extra year.

RULE BOOK

There are several differences between the rules in college football and the NFL. Here are the important ones: 1) In college, a play ends as soon as the ball carrier's knee touches the ground, even if he slips or dives. In the NFL, a player must be tackled. 2) In college, a player catching the ball near the sideline must have one foot in bounds for the reception to count. In the NFL, a player must have both feet in bounds. 3) Since 1996, tie games in college have been decided by a special overtime period. Each team is given a chance to score from its opponent's 25-yard line. In the NFL, the first team to score in overtime is the winner.

WHO'S NUMBER 1?

How is the national champion of college football decided? Each week during the season, teams are ranked from best to worst in several different polls of coaches and sportswriters. These rankings are based on many factors, including a team's record and the level of competition that it has played. At the end of the year, the two top-ranked teams play each other. The winner is declared the national champion. This tradition started in 1998 when college football began using the Bowl Championship Series (BCS). Prior to that year, the top two teams did not always face each other. Sometimes, that made it very difficult to decide which school was the best.

CONFERENCE CALL

Most colleges are members of athletic conferences. Each conference represents a different part of the country. For example, the Atlantic Coast Conference is made up of teams from up and down the East Coast. Teams that belong to a conference are required to play a certain number of games against the other teams in their conference. At the end of the year, the team with the best record is crowned conference champion (unless the league holds a championship game). Teams also play schools from outside their conference. Wins and losses in those games do not count in the conference standings. However, they are very important to a team's national ranking.

BOWL GAMES

Bowl games—such as the Rose Bowl, Sugar Bowl, and Orange Bowl—are extra games played at the end of each season. Bowl games give fans a chance to see the best teams from around the country play one another. These games are scheduled during the Christmas and New Year's holiday season, so students are free to travel to the cities where bowl games are played. There are now more than 25 bowl games.

Since 1998, the BCS has selected the nation's very best teams and carefully matched them in a handful of bowl games. The BCS chooses the champions of major conferences, as well as other schools with talented teams. The two top-ranked teams meet in the BCS title game for the national championship.

Glossary

FOOTBALL WORDS TO KNOW

ALL-AMERICAN—A college player voted as the best at his position.

ALL-SEC—An honor given each year to the conference's best players at each position.

BOWL CHAMPIONSHIP SERIES (BCS)—The system used by college football to select the best two teams to play for the national championship each season. Before the BCS came along, the national championship was unofficial, and more than one team often claimed they were the best.

FIELD GOAL—A goal from the field, kicked over the crossbar and between the goal posts. A field goal is worth three points.

FIESTA BOWL—The annual bowl game played in Glendale, Arizona. The first Fiesta Bowl was played in 1971.

GATOR BOWL—The annual bowl game played in Jacksonville, Florida. The first Gator Bowl was played in 1946.

HEISMAN TROPHY—The award given each year to the best player in college football.

LINEUP—The list of players in a game.

MOST VALUABLE PLAYER (MVP)—The award given to the best player in a bowl game or in a conference.

NATIONAL COLLEGIATE ATHLETIC ASSOCIATION (NCAA)—The organization that oversees the majority of college sports.

NATIONAL FOOTBALL LEAGUE (NFL)—The league that started in 1920 and is still operating today.

ORANGE BOWL—The annual bowl game played in Miami, Florida. The first Orange Bowl was played in 1935.

RECRUITED—Offered an athletic scholarship to a prospective student. College teams compete for the best high school players every year.

ROSE BOWL—The annual bowl game played in Pasadena, California. The Tournament of Roses Parade takes place before the game. The first Rose Bowl was played in 1902.

SACKS—Tackles of the quarterback behind the line of scrimmage.

SEC CHAMPIONSHIP—The game played to decide the winner of the league. The first SEC Championship was held in 1992.

SEC EASTERN DIVISION—A group of teams located near or along the East Coast. The SEC also has a West Division for teams located further from the coast.

SOUTHEASTERN CONFERENCE (SEC)—The league for schools in South Carolina, Georgia, Florida, Alabama, Mississippi, Louisiana, Arkansas, Kentucky, and Tennessee. The SEC began play in 1933.

SUGAR BOWL—The annual bowl game played in New Orleans, Louisiana. The first Sugar Bowl was played in 1935.

TURNOVERS—Fumbles or interceptions that give possession of the ball to the opposing team.

TWO-POINT CONVERSION—A play following a touchdown where the offense tries to cross the goal line with the ball from the 3 yard line, instead of kicking an extra point.

OTHER WORDS TO KNOW

AGILITY—Quickness and grace.

ANCHORED—Held steady.

ARTIFICIAL—Made by people, not nature.

COMEBACK—The process of catching up from behind, or making up a large deficit.

DECADE—A period of 10 years; also a specific period, such as the 1950s.

DETERMINED—Showing great desire.

DOMINATING—Controlling completely.

DYNAMIC—Exciting and energetic.

FORMULA—A mixture of different ingredients.

INSPIRING—Giving positive and confident feelings to others.

LOGO—A symbol or design that represents a company or team.

MASCOT—An animal or person believed to bring a group good luck.

ORIENTATION—The process of teaching people something new.

PROBATION—Suspension from competing.

RIVALRY—Extremely emotional competition.

TAILBONE—The bone that protects the base of the spine.

TRADITION—A belief or custom that is handed down from generation to generation.

UNDEFEATED—Without a loss.

Places to Go

ON THE ROAD

FLORIDA GATORS
University Avenue & Gale Lemerand Drive
Gainesville, Florida 32604
(352) 375-4683

COLLEGE FOOTBALL HALL OF FAME
111 South St. Joseph Street
South Bend, Indiana 46601
(800) 440-3263

ON THE WEB

THE FLORIDA GATORS   www.gatorzone.com/football
  • *Learn more about the Gators*

SOUTHEASTERN CONFERENCE   www.secsports.com
  • *Learn more about the Southeastern Conference teams*

COLLEGE FOOTBALL HALL OF FAME   www.collegefootball.org
  • *Learn more about college football*

ON THE BOOKSHELF

To learn more about the sport of football, look for these books at your library or bookstore:

  • Roza, Greg. *Football in the SEC.* New York, New York: Rosen Central, 2008.
  • DeCock, Luke. *Great Teams in College Football History.* Chicago, Illinois: Raintree, 2006.
  • Yuen, Kevin. *The 10 Most Intense College Football Rivalries.* New York, New York: Franklin Watts, 2008.

Index

PAGE NUMBERS IN **BOLD** REFER TO ILLUSTRATIONS.

The Team

MARK STEWART has written more than 30 books on football players and teams, and over 100 sports books for kids. He has also interviewed dozens of athletes, politicians, and celebrities. Although Mark grew

up in New York City, as a young fan he followed SEC football. When he was eight years old, he spent 75 cents—three weeks allowance!—on the magazine pictured on page 14. Mark comes from a family of writers. His grandfather was Sunday Editor of *The New York Time*s and his mother was Articles Editor for *Ladies' Home Journal* and *McCall's*. Mark became interested in sports during lazy summer days spent at the Connecticut home of his father's godfather, sportswriter John R. Tunis. Mark is a graduate of Duke University, with a degree in History. He lives with his wife Sarah, and daughters Mariah and Rachel, overlooking Sandy Hook, New Jersey.

One might say that **KENT STEPHENS** was destined to have an interest in college football. His mother chose his name while watching the 1953 Rose Bowl, in which Kent Peters was playing for the

Wisconsin Badgers. Keeping in a family tradition, Kent's niece was named for a Rose Bowl Queen when his sister was searching for a name for her baby born on New Year's Day. Kent is a graduate of both The University of Cincinnati and The Ohio State University, and is an avid fan of both the Bearcats and Buckeyes. He has been the Historian and Curator of the College Football Hall of Fame since 1990. He lives in Elkhart, Indiana with his wife Valerie.